ted nash's studies in high harmonics

for tenor and alto saxophone

T0053229

Contents

ISBN 978-0-634-08266-4

HAL•LEONARD®
CORPORATION

7777 W. BLUEMOUND RD. P.O. BOX 13819 MILWAUKEE, WI 53213

Copyright © 1946 UNIVERSAL MUSIC CORP.
Copyright Renewed
All Rights Reserved   Used by Permission

For all works contained herein:
Unauthorized copying, arranging, adapting, recording or public performance is an infringement of copyright.
Infringers are liable under the law.

Visit Hal Leonard Online at
www.halleonard.com

Introduction

The harmonics of the saxophone are rapidly losing their old identity as "false" or "freak" notes and are coming into their own as true legitimate tones of the saxophone. I began experimenting with them a few years ago merely as a hobby for my own amusement, but as I got into it more deeply I found that they were more than something to have a little fun with; they were a completely serious study in themselves. So, in the hope that I might make it easier for those of you who have experimented with similar ideas, I decided to write a book of principles governing the harmonics, along with finger charts, exercises, and examples of the use of harmonics in choruses. It is my feeling that this material coupled with the right amount of perseverance and determination will be of aid in producing a complete chromatic scale with good tone, intonation and fluency.

Good Luck —

Ted Nash

Preface

There is no reason why the tone quality of the normal register of the saxophone should suffer when attempting to produce a good high register. If anything, the production of the high register should strengthen the embouchure, thereby giving one more control throughout the entire range of the instrument. It is not necessary to use an unorthodox type of embouchure; best results are obtained by blowing naturally. Working towards high register does require more pressure from your jaw and lower lip and it stands to reason that the higher you go, the more pressure there is. For this reason, it is not wise to practice for too long a period on high tones during the practice period, since it can be tiring for the lip in the initial stages. It is much wiser to work at them for short intervals each day.

Best results may be obtained by using an open long lay mouthpiece and a medium or medium stiff reed. (Stiff enough so that it won't close up when extreme pressure is applied and yet not so stiff that the vibrance and flexibility of the tone are sacrificed). You will find that a reed of this strength will respond more satisfactorily throughout the regular register of the saxophone and also for the extreme low subtones as well.

The intonation of various saxophones will differ quite a bit in the high register, therefore I've included in the following charts along with the fingerings that I myself use, some alternate fingerings that will enable you to humor the tone. Possibly none of the fingerings I've given for certain notes will work on your instrument, and if that be the case, just experiment yourself by closing or opening different keys until you find the tone that sounds the most in tune and feels the most comfortable for you.

Most of the fingerings that I use on the tenor saxophone do not apply too successfully to the alto, so I've made out a separate chart for that instrument, and my thanks to Santy Runyon, sax teacher of Chicago for assisting me with it.

INSTRUCTIONS ON CHART READING

This diagram will show you how each key is represented on the charts.

★

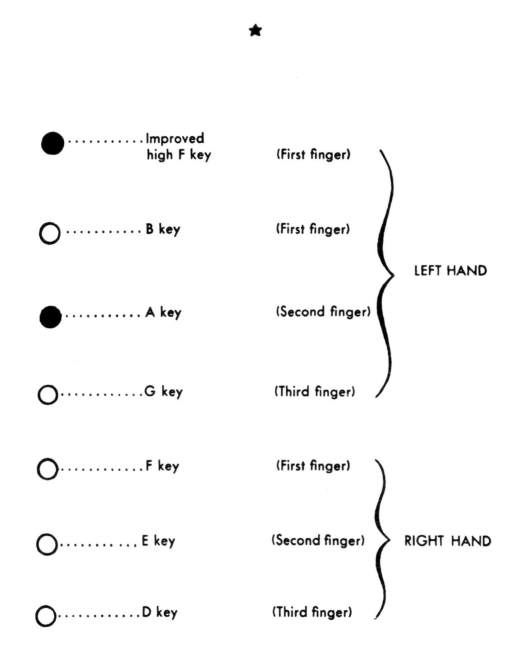

The white circles mean that the key is left open and the black circles mean that the key is closed. The above example, for instance, indicates high F on the saxophone. All additional side fingerings will be noted in each case. The octave key is not indicated since it remains open throughout the whole harmonic scale.

FINGER CHART FOR TENOR SAXOPHONE

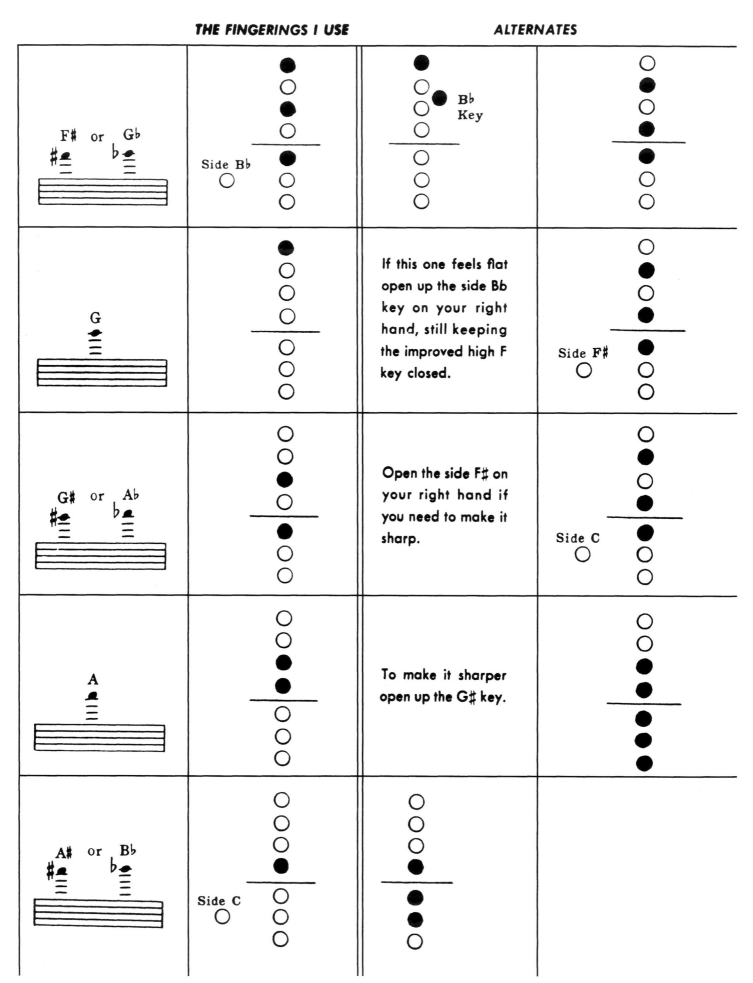

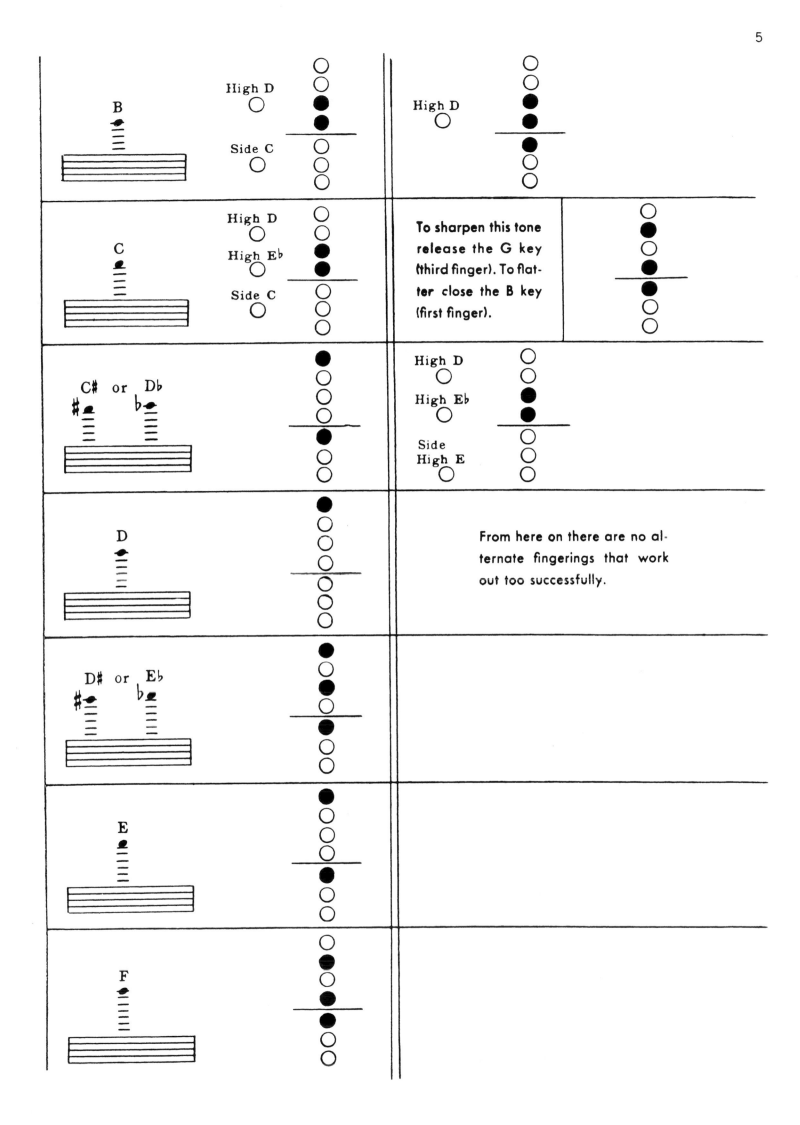

FINGER CHART FOR ALTO SAXOPHONE

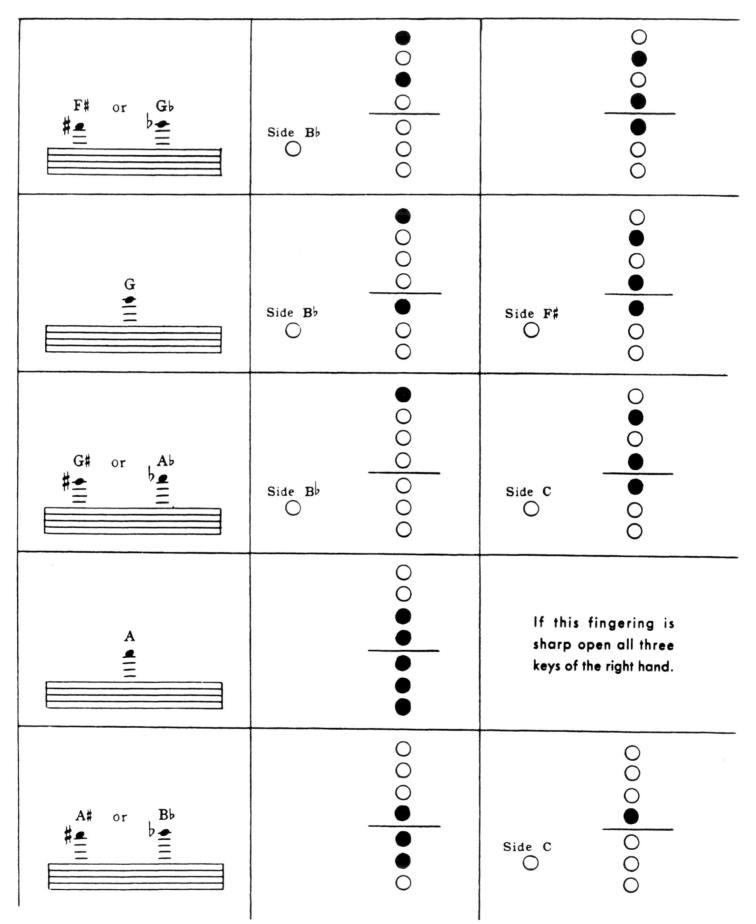

7

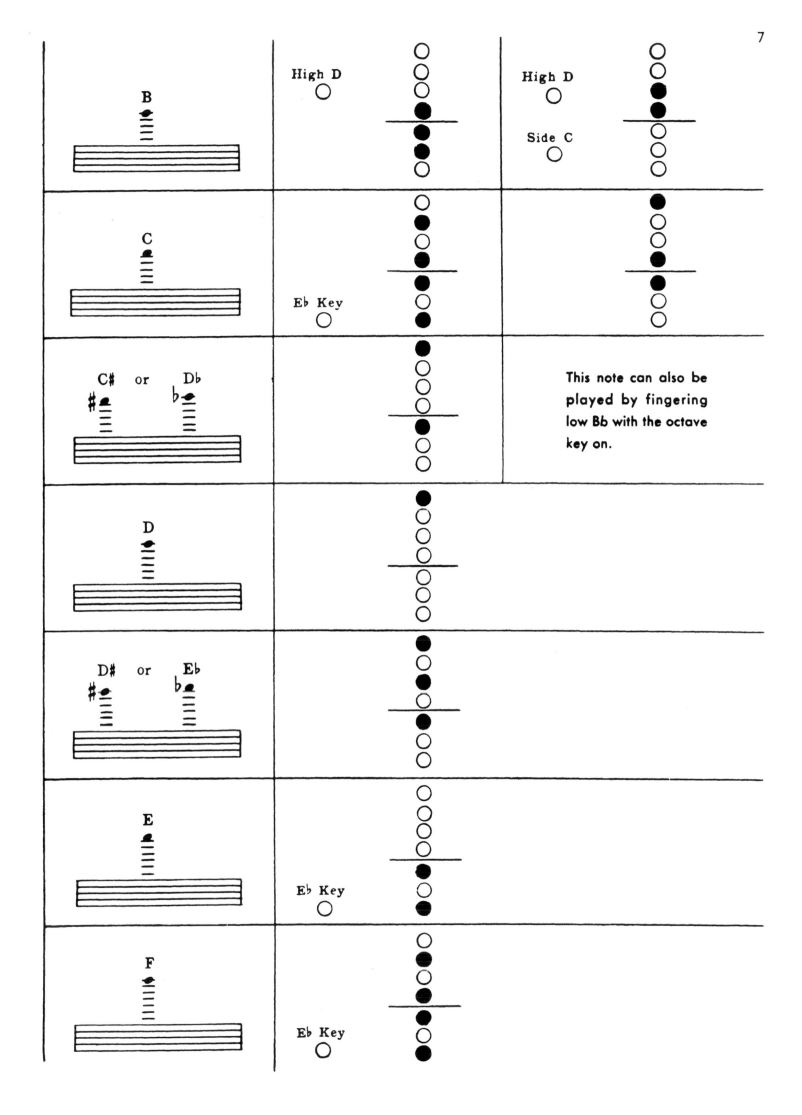

EXERCISES FOR DEVELOPING CONTROL AND FLEXIBILITY

Repeat this exercise going up a half tone each time.

Play each of the following exercises twice. Tongue each note the first time. Slur each note the second time.

In order to make these exercises easier to read, I've cued in the lower octave throughout the whole chapter.

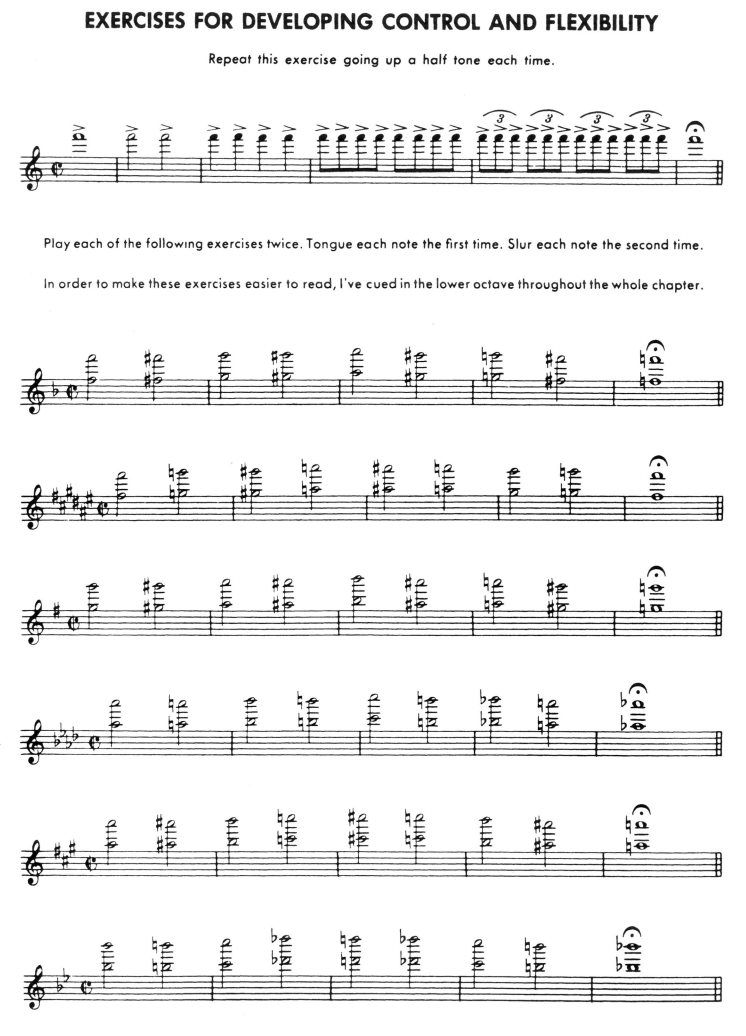

SCALES

3rds & 4ths

5ths

OCTAVES

12

9th CHORDS

EXERCISES USING MODERN CHORD CHANGES

CHORUS PATTERNS

1

2

3

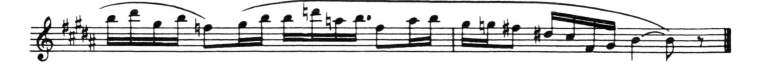

LEAP FROG

Music by JOE GARLAND

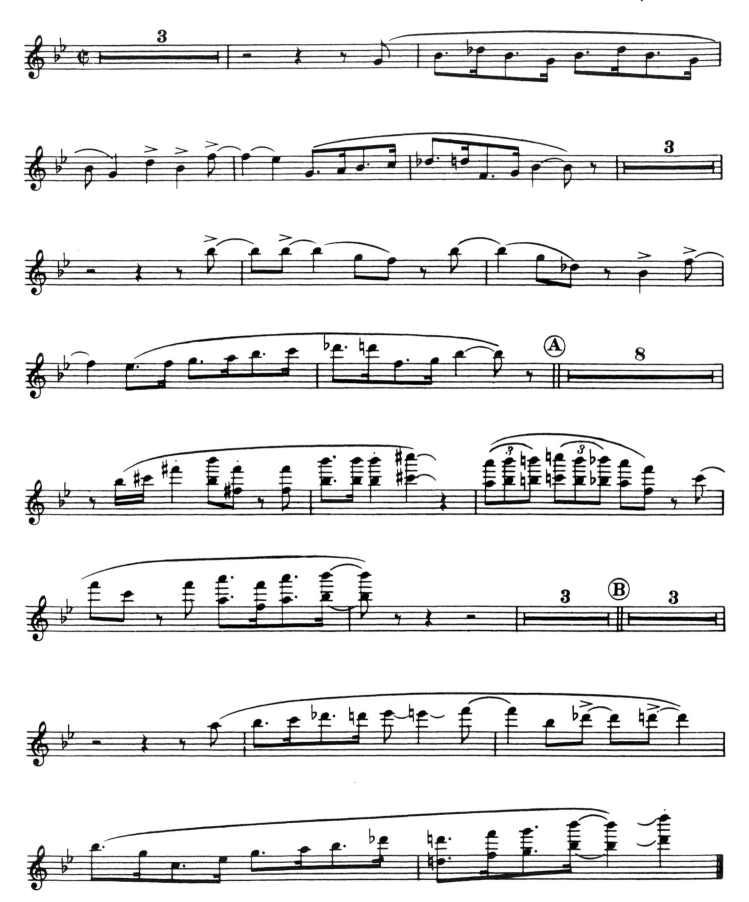

Copyright © 1941, 1942, 1955 UNIVERSAL MUSIC CORP.
Copyrights Renewed
All Rights Reserved   Used by Permission

ALL OR NOTHING AT ALL

Words by JACK LAWRENCE
Music by ARTHUR ALTMAN

Copyright © 1939 by Universal Music Corp.
Copyright renewed, extended term of Copyright deriving from Jack Lawrence and Arthur Altman assigned and effective June 20, 1995 to Range Road Music Inc.
International Copyright Secured   All Rights Reserved
Used by Permission

18

UNDECIDED

Words by SID ROBIN
Music by CHARLES SHAVERS

Copyright © 1939 UNIVERSAL MUSIC CORP.
Copyright Renewed
All Rights Reserved   Used by Permission

I'LL REMEMBER APRIL

Words and Music by PAT JOHNSON,
DON RAYE and GENE DE PAUL

© 1941, 1942 (Renewed) PIC CORPORATION and UNIVERSAL MUSIC CORP.
All Rights Reserved

SALT PEANUTS

By JOHN "DIZZY" GILLESPIE
and KENNY CLARKE

Copyright © 1943 UNIVERSAL MUSIC CORP.
Copyright Renewed
All Rights Reserved   Used by Permission

WICK'S KICKS

By TED NASH

Copyright © 1946 UNIVERSAL MUSIC CORP.
Copyright Renewed
All Rights Reserved   Used by Permission